1

If The Shoe Fits

Cheryl Turnbull

Table of Contents

Introduction

Most women love shoes.

It doesn't matter what kind of women we are we all like our shoes to fit right and look good on us. If we are athletic and outdoors often, we are going to choose shoes comfortable on our feet that wear well. For those of us who love to look good and are willing to endure the discomfort of the high heel shoe we make sure they make our legs look nice. We stand in front of the mirror at the shoe store looking at our foot from all angels, pointing our toes this way and that.

Now, if we love those nice high heels we definitely will not wear them to go on a mile run, or a walk around the block. We will take off those shoes we love so well and slip on the appropriate running or walking shoes.

In this short booklet we are going to see how much we can relate our spiritual life to the shoes we love to wear. Come with me now as we take the first baby step and see if the shoe fits.

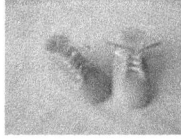

Infant Shoes
For
Baby Steps

I remember there were adorable, cute little shoes available when my children were babies. It was fun purchasing these shoes for my sons and daughters. It was around the time I began having children that cute outfits were designed for boys. When I had my first two children (boys) I had just as much fun dressing them as I did when I had my girls.

Looking back my mom and I did some crazy things. My parents lived in Oklahoma and my husband and I lived in Virginia. Our son, Jonathan, was the first grandchild. My family had a baby shower for me in Oklahoma and my parents and grandmother brought all the clothes with them to Virginia when my son was born. The funny thing was we tried every outfit on Jonathan and took a picture of each one. We did this so they could take pictures back and show my aunts and uncles what Jonathan looked like in each one. I have the pictures to prove this and I'm sure Jonathan would not stand for that now. We all probably have some crazy stories to tell about what we did with our first child.

While our children were infants, and not yet trying to walk, I would put my son's in adorable little baseball outfits with shoes and cap to match. The shoes were just cloth and not normal baseball shoe material. As they grew I put sturdier shoes on them in order to support their feet and ankles as they were learning to walk.

It would not have been appropriate to put the soft shoes, with soft soles and no support, on their feet as they were learning how to walk. They would have fallen because their ankles would not have been supported. The sturdiness of thicker soled shoes and having stronger fabric to support the baby's ankles and feet, are what was needed. These appropriate shoes helped the muscles and bones in the feet develop properly.

As new believers, just learning what living in Christ is all about, we need to realize the necessity of "wearing the appropriate shoes." We can't expect to be ready to teach a Bible class at church or in our home without first being taught thoroughly ourselves. You may have the gift of teaching, but you are not ready to teach just yet. You need to allow the Holy Spirit to help develop your spiritual muscles and bones.

There are those whom we will come in contact with who will have the gift of teaching "baby" believers, and we need to allow them the opportunity to teach us. I Peter 2:2 & 3 says, *"Like newborn babies, crave pure spiritual milk, so that by it you may grow up in your salvation, now that you have tasted that the Lord is good."*

There are many ways to learn without being taught in a classroom. One way is to spend as much time as you can with those who have been walking with Christ a while. Absorb every word they say. Watch their lives. Follow their example. Take them out to lunch or go for coffee. The more you are with them the more you will glean from them.

In John 13:1-17 Jesus gives us an example of leadership influence, or leading by example. He began washing and drying the feet of the disciples. After he finished washing the disciples feet he said, *"...Do you understand what I have done to you? You address me as Teacher and Master, and rightly so. That is what I am. So if I, the Master and Teacher, washed your feet, you must now wash each other's feet. I've laid down a pattern for you. What I've done, you do. I'm only pointing out the obvious. A servant is not ranked above his master; an employee doesn't give orders to the employer. If you*

11

understand what I'm telling you, act like it – and live a blessed life." John 13:12-17 The Message

As new believers it is important to purposefully look for a leader that lives and teaches by example. This type of leader is one who is following Christ's example and will be able to pass on the Christ-like qualities you need in order to spiritually mature. The more time you spend with them the stronger you become, and you will be well on your way to putting on a new shoe. You will be ready to progress in your walk with God and help another "baby" Christian develop in their relationship with God.

Remember do not try to move on to the next level until you are sturdy on your feet. There have been some who have done this and ended up discouraged and given up.

Paul tells us in Ephesians 4:14-15 of The Message, *"No prolonged infancies among us, please. We'll not tolerate babes in the woods, small children who are an easy mark for impostors. God wants us to grow up, to know the whole truth and tell it in love – like Christ in everything. We take our lead from Christ, who is the source of everything we do. He keeps us in step with each other. His very breath and blood flow through us, nourishing us so that we will grow up healthy in God, robust in love."*

It is not meant for us to stay baby Christians for a long period of time. Infants grow faster in the first twelve months than any other time in their life. They are progressing. If they aren't doctors begin doing tests to see why they are not developing normally. If we are not developing and progressing we need to ask ourselves what is wrong with us. Find out what the problem is and work at fixing it.

Paul also tells us in Ephesians to get up and walk, and then he changes his mind and says, no run, on the road God has called us to travel. (4:1-3) We are to run with humility and discipline.

No drama here. No roller coaster Christianity that is up one day and down and depressed the next. We are to steadily pour ourselves out for each other. In verses 4-6 Paul tells us we are traveling on the same road, in the same direction, so stay together. Everything we are and think should be saturated with oneness.

This doesn't mean we are to be clones that look and act identical to each other. We each have been given gifts to use. (Eph. 4:7-13) We are running and traveling in the same direction, but God has a different purpose for each of us. Rick Warren's book, "Purpose Driven Life" is excellent for helping you find purpose. We are each called to expand the Kingdom of God with the gifts, talents and abilities He has given us.

God doesn't expect us to give up things we enjoy doing when we give our lives over to Him. It is just the opposite. He wants to use those abilities and the things we enjoy to reach generations and develop the Kingdom of God. We are given these abilities to advance His ultimate purpose.

We see in Ephesians 4:13-16 that we are to work together until we are all *"moving rhythmically and easily with each other...fully mature adults, fully developed within and without, fully alive in Christ. No prolonged infancies among us, please. We'll not tolerate babes in the woods...God wants us to grow up...like Christ in everything...His breath and blood flow through us, nourishing us so that we will grow up healthy in God, robust in love."*

So what does all that mean? It means that we are to allow the word of God, teaching from our pastors and leaders, and daily conversations with God develop and mature us into the person He desires of each of us. Those who have accepted Christ should understand this principle in their own spiritual development. It is very sad that many Christians never grasp this point and never really mature to the level God has for them. They may have been a Christian for several years, but have never matured.

Just as babies do not stay babies – and yes, they are cute and cuddly and we enjoy them – we are not to stay baby Christians. If we were to allow toddlers to keep their cute ways, when they were clearly defying authority, they would turn out to be rebellious teenagers.

It is hard to correct a two year old when they look at us with innocence, daring us to tell them no, when they are clearing testing our authority. We must, though, in order for them to mature and develop their character and become the adults they should be. As parents and adults we do things and make decisions for our children that will help them, not hurt or deter them.

It would be wise to take this same concept into our spiritual lives. Baby Christians are so "cute" in their innocent beliefs and their walk with Christ. They are excited about this new life they have been born into. They are going to do some amazing things for Christ as they develop and mature.

As "parent" Christians we need to allow baby Christians to grow. Help them learn from their mistakes, but we need to be very careful not to squelch the excitement they have. We should lead and guide them into the oneness Paul talks about in Ephesians chapter four. As "parent" Christians be very careful to make sure we stay fully alive in Christ. Again, take our example from Paul.

We see new believers with all their excitement and we smile. Some people even say, "Oh, they'll calm down after they've been a Christian a while." Why does that have to be the case? May those who have been on the Christian journey a while learn from the new Christians. Take their enthusiasm and excitement and turn it into a powerful force for the Kingdom of God!

He was in prison while writing the letter to the church at Ephesus. He was not allowing imprisonment to deter him from the call of God on his life. He was helping develop believers in Christ. *"God can do anything, you know – far more than you ever imagine or guess or request in your wildest dreams! He does it...by working within us, his Spirit deeply and gently within us."* Eph. 3:20

Paul was an amazing man. God had completely changed his life. He went from persecuting, to persecuted. He once had a passion to destroy and kill the church. God helped him redirect that passion and energy to growing the church. Here he was in prison, much like the ones he once was determined to put Christians in, encouraging the Ephesians to be strong and fully alive in Christ. Our purpose is to be strong, fully alive in Christ, and motivating other's in their faith.

Paul was determined to see these baby Christians develop into mature individuals. In fact he was insistent in Ephesians 4:17 that there was to be no "going along with the crowd." They were to do what God expected, not what the popular crowd was doing. He goes on to say in

16

verses 22-24 that we need to get rid of everything that has to do with our old lifestyle and take on an entirely new way of life. A life that is renewed from the inside and working its way into our conduct, making our character like His.

Paul goes on to admonish us to "watch the way you talk" (4:29). Each word is a gift. So are the words that come out of our mouths gifts or curses? We need to focus on what we say. Are our words helping our hindering? Do they discourage or encourage?

Verses 31-32 tells us to; *"make a clean break with all cutting, backbiting, profane talk. Be gentle with one another, sensitive. Forgive one another as quickly and thoroughly as God in Christ forgave you."* When we are new Christians we will have to work hard at changing our words because they were a part of our language for so long, but we can do it. Make sure that, we more mature Christians do not look down on a new Christian because of their language. Understand they are developing into the person God has called them to, and people will be able to get rid of the old way of life at different paces. So be patient and allow God to work.

As we finish this chapter on Baby Shoes I would like us to ask ourselves the following questions. Really think about them and ask God to help you be honest with each one. By doing this I believe it will help you move on to the next chapter that speaks about the Classic Shoe.

Who are we really? Are we living a "fully alive" life that Paul was talking about? Exactly where are we in our growth as a Christian?

As new babies in Christ, come to the understanding that each day is going to bring new and exciting opportunities for development. You are going to have the opportunity to use your abilities and gifts in ways you never even imagined before you accepted Christ.

Don't be like the person who has been in church for years, but has not spiritually matured. These are people who complain about insignificant things in church. They make a big deal about lights, carpet color, or the music being too loud. Or, there are those who allow the complainers to upset them and decide they are not going to attend church at all and go on their way, sometime not ever stepping in church again. Both people are at fault and have not allowed the Holy Spirit to help them overcome their struggles.

Every believer needs to make it a priority to grow past these differences and mature to a new level in Christ, developing into a Classic Christian. One way to help you progress is "bring a friend on board." Invite someone you know who is not a Christian and help them get to know Christ. This helps you because you will definitely want

18

to develop your own spirit so you can help your friend. You will not want them to develop faster than you! You will be well on your way to becoming a Classic Christian.

Study Guide

1. Think back to your first child...what crazy thing did you do with him or her?

2. What crazy thing did you do as a new believer?

3. What crazy thing did you do when you were first filled with the Holy Spirit or called into ministry?

4. Did you stop doing it? Why or why not?

5. Do you consider yourself a baby Christian?

6. Do you find you go up and down in your spiritual excitement?

7. Find two scriptures to memorize that will help you in your down times.

8. What can you do to develop a spiritual growth plan?

9. Put your personal time with God in your organizer for the first 30 days. This will help you develop a good, healthy habit.

10. Make a list of what you want to see God do for you over the next 30 days. List some of the things you need to change or get rid of in your life.

Classic Style
For
Classic Living

The authentic Christian is one who lives a transparent Christian life; not fake, not pretentious, not exaggerated. They understand the Bible for what it is and live accordingly. They look good. People are glad to be around them. They are not obnoxious and embarrassing to be around. They are classy and sophisticated.

The classic Christian is like the classic shoe you can wear with anything and it looks good. It never goes out of style. The classic Christian will never go out of style. They look good anywhere, with anyone. They are not offensive, yet they do not compromise their beliefs. Others respect them to their face and behind their back. In fact there have been times when non-believers have looked out for and protected a true, authentic, classic Christian.

The Message says in Matthew 6:1, *"Be especially careful when you are trying to be good so that you don't make a performance out of it. It might be good theater, but the God who made you won't be applauding."*

A great example of a true classic Christian is Billy Graham. He is authentic to the core and has never compromised his beliefs. He also has seen the need to reach generations and has reflected this in the meetings he has conducted and passed the baton on to his son.

God wants us to be authentic and genuine. When we are in classes at school, in college, or on the job what do others see in us? What do we act like when we are shopping, playing sports, or just chillin' with friends? Are others seeing an authentic, classy Christian or a person trying their best to fit in by compromising their beliefs in words that are said and actions done? God does not expect us to be rude, but others need to know what we stand for.

A Classic Christian has the burning passion to share their faith and belief in Christ. They do not hold it in. They welcome the opportunity to encourage someone to know Christ, or encourage a believer in their walk with Christ. The scripture in Ephesians 5:16 is in the forefront of their mind, *"So watch your step. Use your head. Make the most of every chance you get."* The Message

I think of the Apostle Paul as another great example of a classic Christian. He was the epitome of classic Christianity...Jewish to the bone. For a taste of how Paul might have grown up read Beth Moore's book; "To Live

22

is Christ." The book will shed light on a boy growing up and being taught the ways of a Pharisee. It is very enlightening.

Paul called himself a "Hebrew of Hebrews" in Philippians 3:5 (NIV). He challenged anyone who thought they knew more than he regarding religion. He knew how to *act* religious, but when God got a hold of his life he immediately gave up the act and began to *live*. For more about Paul's religious background read Galatians 1:11-17.

He turned the zeal for religious ways, and the religious ceremonies he learned as a child, into an unstoppable force; a force that was not to be reckoned with. He was no longer going to try and stop this move of God, he was getting on board, and putting all his energy and strength into expanding this kingdom God was setting in place.

To become a true classic Christian we need to take a long, intense, look at Paul's life; how he conducted himself, how he shared his knowledge with others, how he motivated, instructed and encouraged those whom he brought on board with him.

He was not afraid. He was determined.

He was not threatened. He was challenged.

He was not timid. He was bold.

Because of his former way of life there were many believers who were afraid of Paul. They were not quite sure they could trust him. Let's use our imagination for a moment...some may have been saying...

"Wasn't he the one that was determined to stop this move and put the believers of *the way* in jail? Now he's one of them and he expects me to follow him? I don't think so."

You might have recently accepted Christ and are so excited about what God is doing in your life. You want to share it with your friends and relatives, but like those in Paul's day they remember the way you were and are not ready to trust you just yet. Don't give up. Paul didn't. He plowed ahead with determination, because he knew God called him.

Don't give up, if this is your story. Dig into the Word. Study Paul's life in the Book of Acts and read the letters he wrote. Draw from his depth of insight and plunge forward. At some point people will see that God has definitely changed you; and what you are sharing is worth hearing.

Although Paul had "grown up" in the church, God desired to teach him personally. Paul had to unlearn all the tradition and all the laws. It was God's desire for Paul to have a relationship with Him. Paul knew everything according to book knowledge; he now needed to get the heart knowledge.

Just because we were born in a religious home and attended church since we were infants, does not mean we really know God. We all have to come to the point where we acknowledge we need to know God personally. We may have even accepted Christ into our heart, as Lord and Savior, but is He really Lord in our life? Is all our learning and acceptance just head knowledge? Have we really given God the open door to our heart for Him to get to know us and us Him?

Be careful to not just do things because others are doing them. Don't accept this way of life because it is the cool thing to do and all "my friends" are doing it. Do it for you and no one else. This is the only time selfishness is allowed in the body of Christ. Have a passion to get to know Christ and the power of His resurrection (Philippians 3:10) as Paul did. Don't take what you have heard for granted.

For three years Paul was in Arabia and Damascus learning by revelation from Jesus. (Galatians 2:18) He was only with Peter for fifteen days and did not see any other apostle during that time except for James. (Galatians 2:19) It was fourteen years later when he met up with Peter again. (Galatians 2:1) Paul got to know Christ personally and he set out to change the world in which he lived.

There was no way he was going to be a bystander in this quest. He was going to actively recruit and train the ones who accepted what he had to say. He was not going to leave them to fend for themselves. He was going to make sure they were adequately taught and cared for.

He developed a relationship with them. He spent time with them. He didn't preach a service or two and leave. He stayed with them days and years. When God felt the people were strong enough He moved Paul on another journey. But, the key is, he stayed connected to them. We see this in the various letters he wrote.

When they were struggling he wrote words of encouragement; when they were straying from living right he brought them back in alignment; and when they were going back to religious living by the law he corrected them.

He always started and ended his letters acknowledging the good in them; except for the Galatians. He opens the letter with his credentials, but gets right to the point. The Message uses the term fickle for the believers in Galatia. (Gal. 1:6) Paul was upset because they were letting the teachers of the Law sway them back to their former beliefs.

This should be a lesson for us. When we have been freed from our ritualistic, traditional routines, to an intimate, one on one relationship with God, do not be tempted to go back. Do not be tempted to just go to church for the sake of going to church. Move forward. Go expecting to receive from God. Use your abilities to enhance the body of Christ within your particular church.

That is what a true Classic Christian is all about...living what they have learned. Share your faith. Be passionate about your relationship with Christ. People will see the passion and want what you have. Develop relationships with those around you and help them grow in their faith.

From the moment the Classic Christian wakes up in the morning, until the moment they lay their head on the pillow at night, they are alert to "God moments" that will cross their path. As believers and followers of Christ this should be a priority in our life. Look for the "God moments." Ask God to help you be alert to how He wants to use you throughout the day.

Take this thought with you...

"I want to be a true follower of Christ that has class, one that looks for 'God moments' to happen."

Study Guide

1. What do you look like? Are you authentic? Are you genuine? Write down a description of yourself.

2. List some classic Christians you have known. What makes them stand out to you?

3. What do others see when they see you?

4. Do you do what Eph. 5:16 challenges us to do? (p18) Do you make the most of every opportunity? How can you improve in this area?

5. What did you think of Christianity before you accepted Christ? Can you turn that around, as Paul did, to an unstoppable force?

6. What can you change in your life that will make you more determined, more challenged and more bold?

7. Do you allow God time to get to know us, or do we rush through our prayer and study time with Him? How can you better develop this in your life?

8. How can you develop relationships around you?

9. Do you find yourself going back to old habits? If

so, what can you do to help yourself stay away from those habits?

10. In your own words describe what you want to look like to others.

Running
With
Determination

Paul tells us in Philippians 3:12-13 of The Message, *"I am not saying I have this all together, that I have it made. But I am well on my way, reaching out for Christ, who has so wondrously reached out for me. Friends, don't get me wrong: By no means do I count myself an expert in all of this, but I've got my eye on the goal, where God is beckoning us onward – to Jesus. I'm off and running and I'm not turning back."*

Let's go back to my two boys and my two girls. When they first started walking they were shaky in their steps. As they became stronger I let them wear tennis shoes or running shoes in order to help their feet develop. They each had a determined and excited look on their face as they continued to progress in their abilities.

My oldest son started running cross country and track in middle school and high school. I never realized there were such a variety of running shoes available to choose from! Some shoes are made for distance running, some for sprinting, some made for rubber tracks, and others made for dirt tracks. It is the same for any sport. Different shoes for different functions within the particular sport.

In our life as a believer we may have a gift and ability that can be used in a variety of ways. The gift of administration can be used to organize a fundraiser for a department in the church. The gift of giving could be used to sponsor the event.

You may be a great distance runner, short distance runner, or a sprinter. God can use those abilities if you allow Him the opportunity. Attend races and ask God for wisdom in how you can share your faith. Don't be obnoxious, but allow the Holy Spirit to lead you in unique ways. One example is to kneel at the start line, bow your head and say a prayer before the race. Have a short Bible study an hour or so ahead of the race to motivate the runners. The sky is the limit. Your imagination will be the only thing to hold you back.

If you use to run, or just run as a hobby or for exercise, maybe you could organize a race once a year for your church in order to raise money for a particular ministry within the church. By getting sponsors and charging a registration fee you are allowing people from outside the church to participate. Doing this helps you reach out to your community and financially help a ministry without asking your local congregation for money.

I learned a spiritual lesson from my son, when he was so involved in racing. I found out when runners are preparing for a race they drink plenty of fluids the day before the race to keep them hydrated. It will not do the runner much good to drink an abundance of water the day of or during the race. It is important to drink ahead of time so they will not dehydrate during the race. Then, following the race they can replenish.

Our spiritual lives need the same kind of hydration. We are in a spiritual race. In order to get through the tough times we need to drink in the Word ahead of time. Do not wait until a crisis situation is upon us, and then decide to read and pray. Read the Word and pray regularly, ahead of time, in order to be ready and spiritually hydrated, for the difficult times that will eventually happen in our lives.

Make the decision to be determined, that you will hydrate your spirit and be prepared for the days ahead, when it will be easy to become dehydrated and discouraged. We are not exempt from problems. If we were we would never learn spiritual lessons. If we are not learning from our problems, then we are not developing normally. We will become handicapped in our faith. Do not allow that to happen. Stay on the right track.

In a long distance race there are always water stations along the way. In this long distance race we are in, if we find we need to replenish at a spiritual water station do so, this will help you finish strong. Our spiritual water stations can be fellow believers. There will be other's who have been in your shoes; they may have experienced the same struggles and are there to help give you the strength you need. Welcome their support.

Don't turn them away just because you don't think you need help. By allowing them to help you, does not mean you are weak. It only means you are human. We all need help at some point in our lives.

Take a moment to think about the race at this point in your life. Are you running with determination, or are your ready to give up? Do you feel as if you can't take another step? Your mouth is dry. You can't seem to get another breath. You don't see any point of refreshment in your path. Take a look around you. There is a great crowd of witnesses cheering you on.

The writer of Hebrews encourages us in this race. After writing Hebrews chapter 11, about all those heroes of the faith, the writer says this in chapter 12:1-3, of The Message:

"*Do you see what this means – all these pioneers who blazed the way, all these veterans cheering us on? It means we'd better get on with it. Strip down, start running – and never quit! No extra spiritual fat, no parasitic sins. Keep your eyes on Jesus, who both began and finished this race we're in. Study how he did it. Because he never lost sight of where he was headed – that exhilarating finish in and with God – he could put up with anything along the way: cross, shame, whatever. And now he's there, in the place of honor, right alongside God. When you find yourselves flagging in your faith, go over that story again, item by item, that long litany of hostility he plowed through. That will shoot adrenaline into your souls!*"

The writer goes on to say in verse 7, "*God is educating you, that's why you must never drop out. He's treating you as dear children. This trouble you're in isn't punishment; it's training.*" When runners are in training they are expected to do all kinds of exercises that will build endurance. In fact, trainers recommend cross training. Swimming helps build up your lung capacity, weight lifting strengthens muscles, etc.

So, you see, we should welcome the struggles. They help us become stronger. I, for one, do not necessarily

35

like struggles! For the longest period of time it seemed as if my family's life was one long conflict. At one point my oldest son and two daughters all had a really hard time with life. I had to keep telling myself God was planning something great for each of us.

Do not ever give up, because when it seems you can't go another step, or the struggle is too tough, the victory is just ahead. Many times we give up right before the breakthrough, missing out on the blessing of God. You don't want to miss out on what God has in store, so press on.

Be as determined as Paul and run with purpose toward the goal set before you. Paul tells us that if we are mature (Phil. 4:15a) we should have this point of view... *"So let's keep focused on that goal, those of us who want everything God has for us. If any of you have something else in mind, something less than total commitment, God will clear your blurred vision – you'll see it yet! Now that we're on the right track, let's stay on it."* Phil. 4:15-16 The Message

Run with determination!

Study Guide

1. Where are you in your race? Are you determined or are you weary?
2. What gift did God give to you? How are you allowing God to use it?
3. How often do you drink in the Word to hydrate your spirit? Once a day? Once a week? Once a month?
4. What can you do to improve your spiritual drink regimen?
5. List some people who have been your spiritual supporters or encouragers in your spiritual journey?
6. What are some of the struggles you have gone through? Be honest, now.
7. Have you allowed the struggles to mature you? What have you learned?
8. Are you a determined runner?
9. What do you need to change in your life to make you determined in your spiritual race?
10. Write down some goals that will help you become more determined and reach your goals?

I'll Take One In Every Color

A few years back my teenage girls and I went crazy on buying flip flops. There was such a great deal going on in one of the stores we could not resist getting a pair in every color! You know we had to coordinate the color of the flip flop with the different summer outfits we had. My husband thought we were crazy. We probably were, but we had fun. It was a mom and daughter memory. Jesus tells us in John 10:10, *"I came so they can have a real and eternal life, a more and better life than they ever dreamed of,"* The Message.

We need those times with our children; moments of just being crazy. Many times we become too serious, forgetting to enjoy our daughters while they are young and impressionable. Our children need to see us when we are having fun and doing things out of the ordinary. That is when they realize we are real and not some person that is untouchable.

I will admit there are times when I act too crazy, or should I say stupid, and my girls look at me with the look only girls can make and say, "Mom, please." Throughout the years I have learned not to take things so seriously. There are times I have to remind myself to chill and enjoy life because I do not want to miss out on the fun times with my family.

We are only going to go through this life once, so why not enjoy it while you can. Sure there are the pressures of making ends meet, but when we lighten up a bit we forget about our worries for at least a moment, and realize we can have fun in the middle of struggles.

I love what Jesus says in Matthew 6:30-34 of The Message, *"If God gives such attention to the appearance of wildflowers – most of which are never even seen – don't you think he'll attend to you, take pride in you, do his best for you? What I'm trying to do here is get you to relax, to not be so preoccupied with getting, so you can respond to God's giving. People who don't know God and the way he works fuss over these things, but you know both God and how he works, Steep your life in God-reality, God-initiative, God-provisions. Don't worry about missing out. You'll find all your everyday human concerns will be met.*

"Give your entire attention to what God is doing right now, and don't get worked up about what may or may not happen tomorrow. God will help you deal with whatever hard things come up when the time comes."

Allow the Holy Spirit to bring out the variety of colors in your life. Don't worry about things. Enjoy life!

The world in which we live can make it quite hard to enjoy life and do what Matthew is telling us in this scripture. It is very hard to not think about what you have or do not have when you live amongst many people who have a lot of material possessions. Trying to teach teenage girls it is ok to not have so much or the most expensive cloths is very difficult when you are in the midst of doing life with those who have the most expensive everything.

It is so important to have a clear mind and the confidence of who you are in Christ Jesus. Help your teenager stay focused on God and what He is doing in their life. While growing up they have to get use to the changes in their emotions as well as physical appearance. This is difficult and we need to ask for guidance of the Holy Spirit during these times. I have asked God many times, "Where is the joy of being with my daughters?"

There have been many times I have wanted to rush through this time and get to the stage of life where we can all communicate with each other and like being around each other again.

Girls especially can let their emotions overtake them and think decisions they are making are from God, but really it is based on their emotions. My husband and I have had many conversations with our daughters regarding this very issue. It is so difficult for them to see and they become frustrated and angry at us, the parent. Believe me the only thing that can get you through is prayer...prayer...and more prayer.

This too will pass. You will, once again, get to the point of having fun and living life in full color, not always feeling so frustrated. So be encouraged. Fun is an attitude. Kick the devil and his attacks right where it hurts...ENJOY LIFE! Tell the devil to take a hike. Read on to find out how you can do just that...

Have you ever gone to your closet and looked at what you have to wear and thought, "I think I'll wear yellow today?" I have done this a few times. If you do this ask yourself why you want to wear the color you chose? Did you choose yellow because it is like the sunshine? If so then make a note to self to spread a little sunshine wherever you go during the day.

How about red? If this is a color you chose then your note to self could be reminding you to be bold about your faith throughout the day.

Now if you chose black, which is the formal business look, make sure your note to self is a reminder to not take yourself too serious on that day. It will free you to be open to God's presence allowing the Holy Spirit an opportunity to use you in a special way that day.

I can not say this enough – ENJOY LIFE! This is very hard to do, especially when going through tough times. Those are the times you need to lighten up the most. In today's society we have a tendency to be too serious. We are in competition to do better than the next person and the only way to relax and have a little fun is by drinking it away with alcohol. That is so sad.

We should be able to forget our problems by giving them over to God, not drowning them out. Doesn't Paul admonish us in I Peter 5:7 of The Message? *"Live carefree before God; he is most careful with you."* The NIV says it this way, *"Cast all your anxiety on him because he cares for you."*

Before you dive into a milkshake, eat a second helping, or whatever you do when you are stressed, try feeding your spirit with the Word of God. Your body is not what needs the extra food, your spirit is crying out for more of God. If a person has just accepted Christ and they have been use to going out for a drink after work to "clear their head" have them try listening to some good worship music or preaching CD. They need to build up their faith and there is no better way to do it than by dwelling on spiritual things.

Before going on in the book think back to when there was less stress in your life. What crazy things did you do? Did you play pranks? Did you just, on the spur of the moment, decide to go on a short trip? Think hard now.

I love to sneak up on people. I did this as a teenager and I have been known to have done this to my children when they were just kids. You may think this is mean of a mom to do, but we all had fun. After the kids had gone to bed I would get down on my hands and knees and creep into their room and jump up at them. Now if they were afraid of the dark I would not have done that, but they weren't, so I did.

Now, I will wait just inside a door if I know they are coming through. I even like to jump out at my husband and get him good. I get so much pleasure out of seeing him jump. I can't help chuckling as I think about it as I write. You know what? Even though I love life I have to remind myself to enjoy life. I can get just as serious as the next person and I have to remember my own teaching.

Life is tough, but you can...

ENJOY IT!

Now go think of something out of the ordinary to do
and do it!

Study Guide

1. What crazy thing have you done lately?
2. What crazy thing have you done with your children?
3. Do they see you enjoying life, or are you too stressed with life?
4. What color best describes you? Why did you choose that color?
5. How are you connecting with your children?
6. What are ways in which you can improve your connection with them?
7. Are you enjoying life? Why or why not?
8. What is keeping you from enjoying life?
9. What do you need to "cast" upon the Lord?
10. If you have not done some crazy, outlandish thing recently make a decision to do something soon. Think about what you want to do and write it down.

Protection
For the
Wounded and Weary

There will be times when we need protection from problems that have come into our lives. We need someone to come along side us and be our help and support. We need someone to be our Abishai. (I Samuel 26) We need someone to be the "cast protector shoe" in our lives.

Abishai was the one who accepted David's challenge to go down to the enemy's camp with him. It was going to be risky, but he was willing to give his life for his leader and friend.

I had a young man in our church come up to me, after an evangelist spoke about the relationship of Abishai and David, and say he was going to be my Abishai. He said, "I've got your back Mrs. T." I needed to hear that from him at the time because we were going through difficult times with certain people in our church. The words he said were wonderful encouragement for me. He went on to attend Bible College and is now a youth pastor.

Let's bring this home to our life. As women we need to be Abishai to our spouse. We need to accept the challenge. Be willing to stand firm and be the support, the Abishai, our husbands need. This is so hard when you are going through tough issues with them. You need to work through the issues and ask God to help you be what you need to be.

How can we be a better support? Do we show others we love our spouse by holding their hand, touching them lovingly, or giving them a kiss? This was something my husband and I had to work at because it was not easy for him to show affection. He came from a great family heritage of ministry, but they lacked showing affection. Our generation was taught to not show public affection. Because my husband was a pastor he felt he shouldn't show public affection, such as putting his arm around me or welcoming me or saying goodbye with a kiss.

We learned a difficult lesson. It is healthy for a congregation to see their leaders show they love each other. I don't mean be all over each other in public. I am talking about a little kiss on the cheek, holding hands, or putting your arm around each other. There is nothing wrong with doing that. We are leaders aren't we?

Leaders can help couples who are struggling just by leading by example.

Doing those things in front of your children is also healthy. They see their parents loving each other. Now, our kids would say something like, "ooo, stop that," but the reality was they liked seeing it, even though it embarrassed them.

If this has been difficult for you and your spouse then talk about it with each other and determine to change the "love atmosphere" in your home. If you need the help and support of someone that is what this chapter is about...the cast protector shoe...the supporter.

There will be times when we will be hurt by people. It is inevitable. We, in turn, will unknowingly hurt someone. It will be during those times we will need someone to put their arms around us and encourage us. We, in turn, may be the one to put arms around a friend who is hurting.

Someone may be quiet and stay away from the crowd because they are dealing with issues in their life. They do not want to "burden" anyone with their problems, so they stay away from people. Ask God to help you be alert to these people. You could be a source of strength to them and may even be the one that keeps them from ending their life.

There are women who have gifts that are not being used to their fullest potential. It could be because they were offended at some point in their life. She may just need a word of encouragement. By helping each woman see the gift she has, and sharing ways she can use that gift, possibilities of ministry will open for her in areas she probably never imagined.

What about helping her see ways in which she can help her pastor's wife? Think for a moment how you, as a woman, can be a help and support to your pastor's wife. Does she need some help with cleaning her house? Does she need a break from the kids? What can you do to be an Abishai to the woman who was called by God to be the wife of your pastor?

It is my opinion that for too long the churches have been much too harsh on the woman God gave to their church as pastor's wife. The people in the church can be nice and friendly, but there is the thought that the wife of the pastor is suppose to do what they expect her to do, not what God has called her to do.

The wife of the pastor and her children have been under very watchful eyes. This has hurt the family for too long. I do see a change taking place, but it is in the larger churches. I would like to encourage women from smaller and traditional churches to help the wife of your pastor and his children stay healthy. Do not scrutinize everything they do. Lift them up. Motivate them to be all God intended for them to be.

This puts undo pressure on the pastor to be the mediator between the two. If the congregation puts boundaries upon the pastor's wife in what she is to do or not to do, I believe they will have to answer to God for those things. The pastor's wife will also have to stand before God on how she fulfilled the calling God placed in her heart.

It is sad to see so many pastors' wives discouraged and not doing what God has called them to because of congregations too determined to keep things as they were and not how they should be.

Pastor's wives have to listen to a lot and take a lot of criticism and judgment because they may not "fit" into the mold the congregation thinks she should fit into. Allow her to be herself. Let her develop the gift God has given her.

Each pastor's wife coming to your church is going to have different gifts and abilities. Allow her the freedom to be who she is in Christ. Take a look at Romans 12:6-8 in the NIV, *"We have different gifts, according to the grace given us. If a man's gift is prophesying, let him use it in proportion to his faith. If it is serving, let him serve; if it is teaching, let him teach; if it is encouraging, let him encourage; if it is contributing to the needs of others,*

51

let him give generously; if it is leadership, let him govern diligently; if it is showing mercy, let him do it cheerfully."

Now look at Romans 12:10, *"Be devoted to one another in brotherly love. Honor one another above yourselves."*

If we take these scriptures to heart we will never be out of alignment with God's will. He has given each of us a gift. If we are doing what verse 10 tells us and honoring each other above ourselves, we should not have a problem with freeing our pastor's wife to become all that God has called her to be and called her to do.

I am reminded of an incident in one of our churches; my son, who was in middle school at the time, was bouncing a basket ball off the wall of our youth room in the church. One of our deacons reprimanded him for doing it because it would hurt the paint on the cinder block walls. My thought, "Be glad the child is in church. Take the ball and bounce it with him. Be a friend." Things like that, the good and the bad, stay with the child and can affect the way they see and do church.

There is so much to do for the Kingdom of God and we need to make sure we are not hindering God's plan by allowing our opinions to override what God wants. My prayer is that each one reading this chapter takes the words to heart. Ask these questions, "Am I stifling my pastor's wife? Am I encouraging her in her calling? What can I do to help her fulfill her calling in my church? How am I encouraging and helping mentor my pastor's kids? Am I putting too much undo pressure on them to perform?"

There are women, children, and adults who have grown up as pastor's kids, in our realm of influence that have been hurt and feel abandoned. Make every effort to be a source of encouragement to them. This could even be your pastor's wife. This could be your pastor's child.

Ask God for ways to be the encourager, the Abishai in their lives.

Do this and expect great things to happen. There will be a freeing of spirit and God will do awesome things among you. Take time right now to take out a sheet of paper or go to your computer and write a list of things you can do immediately. Build on the list and share with others so they can learn. Start a group in your church of women who want to do special things for the leadership of your church.

The sky is the limit to what you can do, especially if you ask God for guidance.

Study Guide

1. Read 1 Samuel 26. What stands out about Abishai in your mind?
2. Do you feel you have been Abishai to your spouse?
3. What can you do to become a better Abishai to your spouse?
4. Has there been an Abishai in your life?
5. Have you been an Abishai to another person other than your spouse?
6. Think of someone you could be an Abishai to, someone to whom you can be a "cast protector."
7. How can you help the women in your sphere understand how to become an Abishai?
8. Are you being the Abishai to your pastor's wife that she needs?
9. What are some examples of how you can be a better Abishai to your pastor's wife?
10. Write your list of ways to be a better encourager.

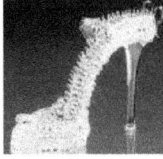

Pretty But not Useful

There are those who think when they get to a certain place as a Christian that they "have arrived." Jesus talks about this in Matthew 6:5. Here's what The Message has to say, *"And when you come before God, don't turn that into a theatrical production either. All these people make a regular show out of their prayers, hoping for stardom! Do you think God sits in a box seat?"*

That is not a good place to be. We may look good. We want other's to look at how great a Christian we are; but we become fragile and could break at any minute. If we are not careful we can become proud and elitist.

We skip a time of prayer or Bible reading because we are running late, or we're too tired. It may be that we think we can go without it for that day, with no problem, but that is where our first line of defense is broken. It is easier for Satan to get into our lives and hinder us.

The next day we have another excuse and before long we haven't had any private time with God for several days; maybe even weeks. We begin losing our temper more easily. We begin laughing at off color jokes, which would have offended us, if we had been having our private time with God.

Attending church service or our women's Bible study group is not as important as it once was. We do not desire to attend the services provided for our spiritual development.

I know people who have not been in church for years because they got out of the habit. There was an excuse, then another excuse, and before long no more excuses, they just didn't hang around anymore with the church friends. In my own life, I went through a time where I did not have any desire for church. I needed someone to be the "cast protector shoe" in my life like I spoke of in the previous chapter.

I had been hurt by church people. I was the wife of the pastor and I did not want to step foot in church ever again! At first I used my handicapped son as an excuse to stay home. When I would go I would go when church started and leave immediately. I did not have a desire to talk to anyone.

I had been our worship pastor and youth pastor, how could that be? My point here is that I started not going and it became easier and easier for me to not want to attend any service at all. We eventually left that church and my husband worked on getting his Doctor of Ministry degree. At first we were so hurt and wounded we did not have a desire for church.

In my heart I did not ever want to have anything to do with church for the rest of my life. I went so far as saying we should just stay home and have church with our family. That was definitely not from God, but I was hurt. It took a while for that wound to heal. In fact, I wasn't totally healed from that experience for three years. We would attend a church in the area in which we lived, but everything about the church reminded me of our previous experience.

It wasn't until our daughter's started having a difficult time that we realized we needed to get in a church where they could be fed and encouraged. We had been attending the one church out of obligation to the pastor because we knew him. Thank goodness God helped us get out of that twisted thinking.

Before I go on I want to elaborate on this for a moment. Many times we attend a church because we feel obligated to the pastor or a friend. It is my opinion that we are going for the wrong reasons. We may even stay at a church as the pastor because we do not know what else to do. That is not a good reason to stay. Seek God. You do not stay at a church out of obligation. You will destroy your family.

My husband and I loved our church. We wanted so much to see them spiritually develop and allow God to use them. They were doing just that, but "circumstances" started happening. My husband and I would encourage each other when one was down and ready to leave. We would stay and see good things happen, but there was always an undercurrent of murmuring from a few people. We were not seeing how it was affecting our children. We wouldn't know this until several years later.

We held out and stayed, but we stayed too long. On some of those occasions we encouraged each other to stay, I believe we needed to encourage ourselves to move on. God did not desire for us to go through what we had to go through. We had choices to make and we made the wrong choices, but God brought us through them and He is helping to develop our ministry into a ministry that is much stronger and powerful.

Be careful.

Be alert.

Listen for the Spirit's voice of change and move.

God has great things for you, so get out there and do them.

When we realized our girls needed help I called the wife of the pastor of the church we had just started attending regularly, and shared with her our girls needs. Her young adult daughter helped my daughters get their lives back on track. I will be forever grateful for her. They began enjoying going to church again.

After a while it wasn't so hard for me to get up on a Sunday morning to get ready for church. I even looked forward to the Sunday night service. Every service the church had was packed with people. God was moving and He was using the pastor and his family to encourage our family in various ways; without them even realizing what they were doing. God was healing deep wounds I never thought would heal. I was once again excited about church and ministry; but, it took almost three years.

If it was hard for me, as a minister and pastor's wife; how much harder, for a normal, ordinary, person to start attending church again?

Those are signs of believers looking good outwardly, but decaying inwardly. We need to be careful, because we will get to a place where we will not be able to handle a particular situation and loose it all together. If you are a woman in ministry please do not build walls around your heart. Allow another woman into your world. This is the first step in keeping you from shattering and breaking apart.

We have been taught to not develop friendships with people in our churches. That is a mistake. Ministry is relationships. You minister better to the people God has placed in your care by developing these friendships. You do have to be careful, but do not let that stop you from being a friend. Also develop friendships with other women in ministry. If other women in ministry are hard to get to know, take the first step. If you want friends you have to be friendly. Go out of your way to develop these relationships. It is important to your health.

I allowed my spirit to get hurt and bitterness set in. I had opened up to someone in our church and considered her a friend. She had issues of her own and my friendship with her hurt me. I had preached about bitterness and hurt, but there were too many hurts I let seep in and stay. If we are not careful our spiritual lives will shatter and break. My spirit was on the road to destruction, but thanks to God, His intervention saved me.

In order for us to look good and not become fragile we need to stay in the Word. Pray continually like Paul admonishes us to do in I Thessalonians 5:17 of the NIV, *"Pray continually."* I knew the Word. I was doing what the Word said.

What I was not giving time to was private, intimate study of the Word for myself. Everything I was doing was for others. That is how it was justified. I prepared sermons and meetings for our youth, but I was not giving time to God for myself. When ministry was taken from me I allowed the hurt to turn into bitterness. I stated this in a previous chapter, but I want to reiterate it here, this is the only time selfishness is allowed; you must have your own private time with God. Get to know Him for yourself, not others.

In Colossians 3:12-17 of the NIV, Paul admonishes us in the right way to live; *"Therefore, as God's chosen people, holy and dearly loved, clothe yourselves with compassion, kindness, humility, gentleness and patience. Bear with each other and forgive whatever grievances you may have against one another...And whatever you do, in word or deed, do it all in the name of the Lord Jesus, giving thanks to God the Father through Him."*

If someone has offended you, forgive them. It was several years before one of the persons that hurt me wrote an email asking forgiveness. I had moved on and God was doing new things in my life, so this came as a total surprise. At first I didn't recognize the person, but after corresponding back and forth I realized who it was and was able to forgive.

If we take these scriptures to heart; keeping others in mind before ourselves, we will not be just a pretty shoe to look at; we will be strong and more like a beautiful Classic Shoe with substance that will last a lifetime.

One of my deepest prayers is that I can, in some way, encourage other women in ministry. I do not want any one of them to have to go through what I went through. If you know of a woman in ministry who has been hurt, or is going through struggles, don't leave her out there alone. Go to her and extend a loving hand. Be a strong shoulder of support to her. Don't let her break. Help keep her strong.

Study Guide

1. Do you look good as a Christian?
2. Do you put on a "show" for others?
3. Are you just going through the motions of church?
4. Have you been offended?
5. Are you letting that offense eat at you like a cancer?
6. Do you need to forgive?
7. Who do you need to forgive?
8. How can you help someone else overcome their hurts?
9. How can you avoid falling into the trap of "pretty, but not useful"?
10. What can you do to move from being a "pretty, but not useful" to "classic" Christian?

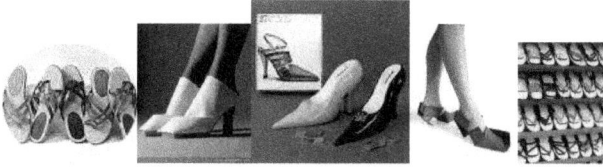

Which Shoe
Am I
Anyway

Just like the shoes we wear, we each have a unique and individual style. We are not all alike. Thank God! We each have a purpose in our church, with our friends, and in life in general. Romans 12:4, 5, talks about the body and its different functions. I once preached a sermon titled, "So You want to be an Armpit?" The whole point of the sermon was getting the body to work together. Everyone is important. We all need each other.

The church needs everyone to participate and do life together, supporting each other. Without the armpit there would be no arm, shoulder, or side. The armpit is important. Without each other there would be no church. The church is not a building; it is the people that live, breath, and work in and out of the building that make up the church body.

The same applies to the shoe illustration. You would not wear Stilletos to run a race. Neither would you wear running shoes to a wedding. You were the shoe that is appropriate for the function.

Where do we fit in? Are we using our gifts appropriately – for the right function?

God has given each of us talents and abilities to use. Are we using them wisely? There will be times that we will be needed to be a shoe of protection to someone. Or, we may need to help a new believer take those first baby steps. Someone has said that "talent most likely will diminish with age, while spiritual gifts seem to improve and deepen with age."

Just because we had a particular gift in the past does not mean we cannot have a different one later in life. God will choose how He can best use us, if we allow Him. He may want to mature us to a new level in Him by using us in a new way. Please, do not ever limit God in what He desires to do in and through us.

Paul's admonition to Timothy is great encouragement for each of us, *"Get the word out. Teach all these things. And don't let anyone put you down because you're young. Teach believers with your life: by word, by demeanor, by love, by faith, by integrity. Stay at your post reading*

Scripture, giving counsel, teaching. And that special gift of ministry you were given when the leaders of the church laid hand on you and prayed-keep that dusted off and in use.

"Cultivate these things. Immerse yourself in them. The people will all see you mature right before their eyes! Keep a firm grasp on both your character and your teaching. Don't be diverted. Just keep at it. Both you and those who hear you will experience salvation." I Timothy 4:11-16 NIV

What are we doing to "get the word out?" Are we stuck in a gift we had in the past and God is waiting for us to open up and not be so stubborn. In the culture we live in today, if we are not willing to change in an instant the culture will pass us by. We have got to be willing to adjust in order for God to use us. If we don't He will find someone who is ready, willing, and able to go now.

Remember the gift God has given you, be open to change. Remember when people prayed for you and you accepted Christ. Remember when God called you to a particular ministry. Cultivate all this and allow the Holy Spirit to use you in your uniqueness.

Several years back one of the youth who was attending a Christian university came home one weekend and told me they did not like a particular worship ministry that had become well known internationally.

The reason he didn't like them was their style changed with whatever was popular at the time.

That is my point. We live in a culture that is changing drastically. If we do not embrace it, without compromising the word of God, we will lose a generation. It is imperative we do whatever it takes to reach every generation, passing on the legacy we have inherited.

Ask Him to give you a hunger for more of Him.

Immerse yourself in what He is doing.

Develop a passion that is deep, that will endure, that will challenge, that will motivate, and that will empower.

Hold on tight to God's spirit and be ready to see the glory of God shine through your life!

Study Guide

1. What is your unique style?
2. How are you contributing to your local congregation?
3. Is your style developing into a different style than before?
4. How are you cultivating your style?
5. Do you have a hunger for more of God?
6. How can you immerse yourself into Him more?
7. List steps you will take to develop a passion for Christ,
8. Be open to whatever it is that God is going to do in your life.

Conclusion

I could not resist this picture. I think I have seen everything! A shoe motorcycle! Can you believe it? My husband loves motorcycles. He had a Harley and we had to sell it a few years ago. He watches TV shows on how they make choppers. When I was searching Google for images of shoes for this book I came across the picture at the top of this page. I told my husband we needed to get that kind of motorcycle next time we bought one. I don't think he liked the idea.

The point of this shoe is to encourage each of us to have fun with who we are in Christ. Let our lives be bursting with life. Jesus said in John 10:10 of The Message, *"I came so they can have real and eternal life, more and better life than they ever dreamed of."*

Are we living up to what God expects of us?

Are we enjoying this life we are living?

Can God look at us and say, "Yeah, she's my girl. She's living life the way I expect her to live." Or does He look at us with hurt and disappointment because we aren't living up to the full potential for which He has called us.

We are all, each one of us, uniquely and wonderfully made. (Ps. 139:13-16) God has many great plans for our lives. Ask Him today to help us begin this awesome race of living on the edge of life; daring the enemy of our soul to attack us.

Begin to determine which shoe you need to wear at any given time. When we realize we are made for specific tasks we show our enemy we know what we are doing. He will then realize it will not be so easy to deter us from our goal.

I would like to end the book with a couple of scriptures: II Corinthians 4:8, 9 *"We are hard pressed on every side, but not crushed; perplexed, but not in despair; persecuted, but not abandoned; struck down, but not destroyed."* NIV; Philippians 4:13, *"I can do everything through Him who gives me strength."* NIV

Come on girls pick your shoes and let's run this race to win!

With the appropriate shoe of course!

About the Author

Cheryl Turnbull was born in Tulsa, Ok where she lived with her family until attending Central Bible College in Springfield, Mo. After attending CBC for four years, majoring in music, Cheryl married Stanley Turnbull and moved to Virginia Beach, Va.

They have lived on the East Coast for the past twenty-five years; in which time, Cheryl received her License to Preach from the Potomac District of the Assemblies of God. During this time she worked as youth pastor and minister of music in the churches in which her husband was pastor. She and her husband have four children, two boys and two girls.

If you would like Cheryl to come and speak for one of your functions she can be contacted via email at hstrymknwmn@hotmail.com or look her up on facebook.com or myspace.com. More information regarding her ministry can be found at www.mentoringwomeninministry.com and www.mentoringwomeninministry.blogspot.com, or you can check us out on Facebook. We have a Mentoring Women in Ministry Group and Blog.

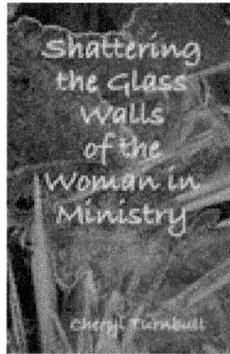

Another Book from

Cheryl Turnbull

The women of today's generation want to know how ministry is done and what is expected of them. Just what does it mean to be the wife of a pastor or woman in ministry? We need to share with them and show them what it means to take our family with us in ministry, without losing them to the world. If you want to be encouraged as a woman in ministry to continue in your journey this is the book for you.

Order your copy today from, www.shatteringtheglasswalls.com.